" ...the figure is the essence of m

ny work, the human content, the emotional link...

...the figure is the essence of my work, the human

ontent, the emotional link..."

# EYE OF THE NEEDLE

## The Textile Art of Alice Kettle

TELOS

First Published in Great Britain 1995

Softback: ISBN 0 9526267 8 0

Hardback: ISBN 0 9526267 9 9

A CIP catalogue record for this book is available from the British Library.

**Telos Art Publishing**

PO Box 125, Winchester S023 7UJ

Fax + 44 (0)1962 864 727

Front cover:
Top: **Blue Nude V (1993)** 11" x 15", 28 x 39cm, *Private Collection*
Bottom: **Niagra (1995)** 37" x 25", 92 x 63cm, *Private Collection*


**Medium:** *Machine embroidery*
*in cotton, silk, rayon and metallic thread, unless stated.*
*All dimensions given are approximate: height x width (x depth)*

**Man and Two Birds** (1992)
78" x 31", 200 x 80cm

## Preface

Goldsmiths' College Department of Embroidery and Textiles has, since the 1950's, attracted students of exceptional ability. Interviewing students for admission brings moments of delight and every now and then a student appears whose work convinces from the first piece seen, and there's a shiver of excitement. Alice's interview was one of those times of delight – this gently spoken, seemingly fragile young woman opened up her portfolio to reveal a series of quite magical paintings. Very small in scale, vibrant in colour and peopled with small figures, they described an intimate, imaginary world. As I recall, there was only one somewhat primitive embroidery, but even in that state it showed that Alice had an intuitive understanding of the medium of thread and fabric – she was in.

I anticipated small-scale, hand-embroidered work from Alice – how wrong I was! This gentle person had an inner core of toughness, physical stamina and a huge ambition for her work. The industrial sewing machine became her natural tool, and fabrics were pounded into submission as her imagination soared. She explored the world of historical embroidery and released herself from the constrictions of the rectilinear format. Embroideries began to flow across the wall and onto the floor. This discharge of energy has continued and she has never stopped working.

The embroideries are always figurative, and many layers of reference are contained within each piece. They reveal subtleties of imagination and execution which refute any notion of embroidery as "mere decoration." Ten years after leaving college Alice has a substantial body of work behind her and a growing international reputation as an artist. From this point on we can look forward to developments in her work which may surprise and will surely delight.

**Audrey Walker** MBE

*Head of Embroidery and Textiles, Goldsmiths' College (retired)*

# THE EVOLUTION OF A PERSONAL STYLE

## A PERSONAL STYLE

Jennifer Harris

**Alice Kettle's** textile art is firmly anchored in an English tradition which goes back to the widely acclaimed medieval church embroideries, known as *opus anglicanum*, and continues through William Morris' nineteenth-century designs for large embroidered hangings imitating medieval tapestry. Technically and conceptually, however, her work belongs unequivocally to the end of the twentieth century, for she is using modern industrial machines and new fibres to express contemporary experience.

Recent years have seen a new kind of art emerging-one which uses traditional craft media, with integrity, to express fine art sensibilities. Her background in painting, together with her discovery that textile art is the medium with which she is most comfortable, make Alice Kettle one of the prime exponents of this new art.

**People in Boxes** (1984)
Gouache, 29" x 22", 74 x 56cm
*Private Collection*

Born in Winchester, Hampshire, in 1961, Alice's background was academic rather than artistic. The middle of three sisters, she was brought up in the male-dominated atmosphere of the public-school Winchester College. Her father was a house-master and French don, and the family shared a boarding house with fifty boys. Her mother's influence, however, was profound, and Alice recalls her showing a passion for textiles that went well beyond an ordinary domestic interest in home dressmaking and house furnishings. She regularly took the girls to textile degree shows at Winchester School of Art, and encouraged them to use their time at home creatively. According to Alice, fabric remnants would *'spill out of every drawer you opened'*, and one of her first hangings, **Harlequin Madonna**, was inspired by memories of a 'Kitchen Madonna', a project carried out at home under her mother's supervision when she was five or six .

After A-levels, a sense of guilt at disappointing her father's academic ambitions steered Alice in the direction of a traditional university rather than an art school, and in 1979 she went to Reading University to study Fine Art. She soon discovered a talent as a colourist rather than as a graphic artist, but during the foundation year, which combined theoretical with practical studies, the tragic death of her mother in a car crash interrupted Alice's course, and she found it a struggle to complete the remaining years in the painting studio.

The trauma also had an impact on her style: the large canvases in a bold, Abstract Expressionist style of the early period at Reading were replaced by smaller, more introspective works which now included figures. Initially these were self-portraits, or portraits of people who were important to her at the time. Gradually they became more impersonal, though invariably reflecting her own emotional state. Alice sees these early figures as being confined within boxes, either drawn literally or represented by the edges of the canvas itself. What is less clear is whether, with the passage of time, the idea of containment was not more inhibiting than comforting.

The move from abstraction to figurative work was to prove significant, for it is difficult now to imagine Alice's work without the human element. Although the figure no longer has the intensely autobiographical degree of involvement with the artist which it had in her early pieces, it still remains the central focus of Alice Kettle's work:

*"If my work became totally abstract I believe it would fragment. The figure is the absolute essence of the work, the human content, the emotional link for me as an artist."*

After switching from painting to embroidery Alice spent the first few months exploring the means of expressing gesture in this new medium, a period marked by a whole series of figures standing, sitting, lying, or kneeling. Though an exploration of movement and gesture, it is also notable that these early embroidered figures show no more willingness than their painted predecessors to escape the confines of the box/canvas.

It was the move from painting to embroidery which would ultimately free Alice from the constraints of the canvas. She went to the postgraduate textile degree show at Goldsmiths' College (University of London) in 1985, the year after she graduated from Reading, and vividly remembers her sense of excitement. The emphasis at Goldsmiths' has long been on textiles as a fine art, with a bias towards ideas and intention rather than technique. Alice was determined to apply for the postgraduate diploma, despite having only one piece of textile art in her portfolio. To her great delight she was accepted.

**Girl in her Room** (1985)
Gouache, 28" x 20", 71 x 52cm

*"This piece was my very first embroidery, the only textile I had to show at my Goldsmiths' interview. I had taken out a book on embroidery from the local library, and I experimented by trying to translate a painting I had already done. I put everything to hand through the sewing machine, even large pipe-cleaners and feathers. It took over a month."*

**Untitled Embroidery** (1985)
14" x 20", 36 x 51cm

Although in principle the whole range of textile techniques was open to her, Alice quickly realised that stitch was the medium that best suited her way of working. She frankly admits that her strength does not lie in the forward planning and careful thinking through of technical processes required by, say, dyeing and printing. Stitch, on the other hand, is more immediate and machine stitching in particular appeared to suit her more intuitive approach. She never seriously considered hand embroidery because the work is so laboured, making it near impossible to put in broad, painterly sweeps of colour. Machine embroidery allowed her to mix colours and apply strokes in much the same way as she had done in paint but was, she discovered, more liberating than working in oil or gouache.

A more obviously tactile medium, embroidery allowed Alice finally to break free from the two-dimensional, rectangular surface. She found that by repeatedly stitching over certain areas, her method of 'overpainting', rippling three-dimensional surfaces and shadows were formed; and that the use of metal threads produced interesting glistening textures which she had never experienced with paint:

*"It was as if the canvas itself was also changing, rather than me just putting more and more onto the surface of it."*

Embroidery was liberating also in the sense that Alice felt released from the weight of the painting tradition. Embroidery as an expressive medium, as a means for the exploration and realisation of ideas and feelings as opposed to a purely functional skill, is a relatively modern phenomenon. It has its roots in the Arts and Crafts movement of the late nineteenth century, though only since the 1960's have the technical boundaries of embroidery been pushed outward, revealing the expressive possibilities of stitch as a fine art medium. For Alice the discovery was exhilarating. Her background in painting, together with her remarkable physical stamina, gave her the confidence and strength to cover large areas in a way that is rather alien to a medium with its roots in hand-work. She was able to marry an innate feeling for textiles with the painter's concern for colour and line. She felt that, at last, she had found her medium and her identity.

Needless to say, Alice's year at Goldsmiths', which ended in a highly successful degree show and a special commendation for her work, was not without its anxieties. The problem was both technical and aesthetic: she needed to acquire competence on the machine which would allow her to understand the possibilities of the medium, whilst seeking a new means of expressing her ideas.

After one particularly tough critical analysis of her work, she decided to consider the formal and pattern-making aspects of textiles. She began to look at more stylised work and formal gesture, in, for example, Russian icons, medieval tapestry and Giotto's painting. At the same time she would spend whole days experimenting with the machine, pushing it to its limits, determined to make it work for her.

**Two Women** (1986)
52" x 64", 132 x 167cm

*"At the back of my mind were the lessons learnt from painting: to vary the types of marks and the scale of brush strokes, to balance bold areas with dynamic lines. But this was a different kind of mark-making, more like constructing. I remember feeling a mixture of excitement and frustration at how slow it was compared to painting. I got quite carried away with the pleasure of handling material, of watching bold lines of thread appear. But getting the machine to work against its will was a struggle."*

A feverish period of work between April and June 1986 resulted in the three large hangings which she put in her degree show, **Harlequin Madonna**, **Eve Falling from Grace**, and **Two Women**. All are characterised by their mosaic-like, patterned surfaces and are dominated by large female figures who sensuously twist and float in a gently undulating, patterned space. The influence of the medieval art which Alice had been studying is evident in their serene expressions and stylised gestures, and in the choice of such feminine icons as Eve and the Madonna. Their seeming weightlessness lends a puppet-like quality to the figures, an aspect which is re-stated more consciously in a slightly later hanging, **Pulchinella** (1987).

Though the figures in these hangings are still contained within the frame created by the 'canvas', Eve engages more dramatically with it by her fall through space into a worldly state. The hanging begins as a wall-piece but spills onto the floor almost like a carpet, the convergence of the two formats emphasising a fluidity both real and implied by the title. That same year **Eve** was selected for the exhibition Stitched Textiles for Interiors at the Royal Institute of British Architects, attracting further critical attention to Alice's work. Since then she has continued to show work on a regular basis in both solo and selected group exhibitions.

The technique which Alice developed during those final weeks at Goldsmiths', her method of using the sewing machine as a painting and drawing tool, has become the hallmark of her work. In her hands the machine becomes an expressive as well as a mechanical tool. The needle is freed by removing the foot and setting all the dials to zero. Then Alice 'draws' by moving the fabric around beneath the needle, almost as though when drawing, the pen were fixed in the needle and you moved the paper. The tension between the upper thread (in the needle) and the lower (in the spool) is used to mix colours and develop shapes in the surface, while the balance between the two is changed continuously. Two or more threads may be used on top.

Alice 'applies' the stitching in much the same way as she used to apply paint, building up layer upon layer of different threads, and frequently re-defining individual lines and shades of colour. Often, particularly with the figures and faces, the thread she uses is too thick to fit through the needle so she winds it on to the lower spool and works `blind' from the back of the cloth.

Even without the added complication of working from the back, viewing the progress of work on the large hangings is difficult because so much fabric is being manipulated under the narrow arm of the machine. Alice solves the problem by taking the work out and reviewing it as often as is practicable. With the smaller pieces this can be done frequently but, with the large hangings which are difficult to manoeuvre back into the machine, a lengthy period of contemplation in the morning, before she starts work, often suffices:

The author with the central panel of
**Three Caryatids** (1988-9)

*"It might keep me going for the rest of the day because I've absorbed enough information. The work is quite slow and there aren't really vast changes you can make over a day, when you're working on that scale."*

This method of working also means that the artist has to be prepared to move sections, re-work areas and re-draw shapes. Inevitably, there are days when she is discouraged by the lack of progress but, equally, other regenerative periods of covering ground in a satisfactory way.

People are often surprised to learn that Alice does not keep sketchbooks and work from those. She tends to work straight on to the fabric, with little or no preparation, accepting that 'cutting and pasting' and constant re-stitching are part of her working process. She will generally have an initial sense of the figure on starting out but the precise image only emerges as the work progresses. It is, in all senses, a very organic process. Typically, with a large hanging, Alice will begin by stitching an outline of the figure, but because the subsequent stitching creates so much tension over the surface of the fabric, the figure invariably becomes contracted. Then she will insert a new piece of fabric and work over that. Conversely, she may cut a piece away if, for example, the fabric has become so thick with stitching that it is unworkable, and patch in a new piece. As a result a piece of work is rarely abandoned in its entirety. **Three Caryatids** (1988-9) are a prime example of this 'cutting and pasting' technique as they were worked on over such a long period of time.

After leaving Goldsmiths', Alice returned to Winchester, working at first from the Design Workshops at Winchester School of Art, then later from an attic room in her father's house. As she grew more confident in her handling of the sewing machine she gradually developed a clear voice. She produced a large body of work during 1987-88, all incorporating a female figure, but, in comparison with the Goldsmiths' hangings, they are striking above all by their heightened sense of dynamism. The figures jump, dance or stretch and now frequently break out from their spaces instead of being contained by them. Alice explains that:

**Dancer II** (1988)
31" x 22", 89 x 59cm

*"because there was so much movement in the surface of the work, to have a static figure seemed almost to contradict what was happening with the materials."*

What is also notable is that they are physically less ethereal than the earlier figures; they exude strength and poise, a reflection of the artist's own growing self-confidence.

Critics seeking to discover in Alice's work the influence of other artists have mentioned Klimt and Hundertwasser in connection with the early, patterned work. Certainly, in pieces such as **Eve Falling from Grace** and **Harlequin Madonna** one can find echoes of the ornamental qualities and the lavish use of gold and silver leaf in Klimt's more mature painting, such as the portrait of *Adele Bloch-Bauer* (c. 1907) or the mosaic designed for the *Palais Stoclet* (completed 1911). In these works the figures and ground are virtually indistinguishable, achieving the sort of decorative unity for which Alice was striving in her first large hangings. There is too an iconic quality to Klimt's portraiture which is called to mind by the facial expressions of Alice's female figures.

**Blue Nude V** (1993)
11" x 15", 28 x 39cm
*Private Collection*

The references to Klimt are largely sub-conscious, the result of Alice's decision to explore the pattern-making aspect of textiles. She is more conscious of a debt to painters such as Botticelli, whose graceful, feminine figures were an early influence, and Howard Hodgkin, whose direct, decorative vigour and use of colour to convey memory or emotion have great resonance for her. She shares with Hodgkin the quest for a rich balance of pattern, colour, composition and elusiveness of content. Like him, too, she does not draw, but works by making marks in pure colour, he in oils, she in thread. However, the overriding influence on Alice's development as an artist has surely been that of Matisse:

*"I feel more in tune with Matisse than with any other artist. I go back to him all the time."*

In works such as *The Dance* (early 1930s), where the figures spring and tumble across the space, or in the *Blue Nude* series of 1952, Matisse appears to be searching for that balance of figure and ground which has been the concern of all of Alice's work since leaving Goldsmiths'. The *gouaches découpées* (painted paper cut-outs) which began as a device in Matisse's working process but became the substance of his art in the final years of his life, have a particular resonance for Alice:

*"I can see parallels between embroidery and the cut-outs. In embroidery you are putting two threads together, which you can't mix as you can paint. You can't physically join them together, you can only place them next to each other. It's exactly what Matisse was doing with the paper cut-outs, using scissors to create gesture. And, as with embroidery, you can read them as purely decorative, but there's so much more to them than that."*

Towards the end of the 1980's Alice began to work on a series of huge composite hangings which pushed her physical and mental stamina to the limits. In marked contrast to the intense dynamism of her dancers, jumpers and varied nymphs, **Three Caryatids** (1988-9) and the slightly androgynous male figure in **Creation** (1990-1) are statuesque and more contemplative. **Three Caryatids** (the title is a reference to the female figures in Classical architecture used in place of columns) was inspired by monumental stone carvings seen by Alice on a journey which she made to Eastern and Central Turkey in 1988. At the end of a day spent climbing a mountain called Nemrut Dagi, she watched as the setting sun *"bathed the dull grey stone heads in a surreal orange light, glowing and shimmering."* The embroideries evoke the memory of these Classical remains, and also convey something of the emotions which the scene aroused. The figures communicate energy and quiet dignity, strength without aggression.

**Creation**, a composite work made up of four hangings, was also a response to a journey, this time to India, where Alice went in 1989 to visit textile-making centres. The shimmering quality of the light in India was the primary inspiration behind the embroideries, and is emphasised by the rich, gold tones with which the hangings are suffused. However, the work is intended also to convey something of the beauty and resilience in the face of desperate poverty of the people themselves, and to celebrate Man as God's creation. **Creation** highlights the spiritual dimension which is present in much of Alice Kettle's work.

**Creation** (1991)
*Detail*

**Happy Stumpers** (1993)

*4" x 10", 10 x 25cm*

*Private Collection*

Both **Three Caryatids** and **Creation** now hang in public spaces, in an art gallery and library respectively. Their scale is arresting, the magnitude of the projects breathtaking. They totally subvert the common pre-conception of embroidery as small scale and painstakingly executed, and capitalise on the ambiguity between the primitive and monumental on the one hand, and the use of precious silks and metal threads on the other. Because of the labour intensive qualities of the medium and the domestic connotations of stitched textiles many people still see embroidery as a conservative medium. Works such as **Three Caryatids** and **Creation** seriously challenge that view.

Alice's first child, Poppy, was born in January 1991, a few days after Alice completed **Creation**. A second daughter, Tamsin, soon followed in July 1992. Inevitably, the demands of children have meant that Alice's working day has become fragmented. However, she determined from the outset to arrange for childcare that would enable her to keep on working and, like many working mothers, she has discovered that when time allows she can work in a very focused way. Motherhood has had little impact on Alice's work stylistically, although the pleasure she derived from the birth of her first baby and the constraints of working around an infant were largely responsible for a series of smaller-format, framed embroideries on folk themes, groups of **Cherry-Pickers**, **Happy Stumpers**, and the like.

Much of the last three years has been given over to the planning and production of two major commissions, the first an altar frontal for the Holy Sepulchre chapel in Winchester Cathedral, the other a series of six large panels on an Indian theme for the Curzon Room aboard P&O's luxury cruise liner, *m.v. Oriana.* The discipline of sewing to a drawn design is not an easy one, and in some ways tends to inhibit Alice's intuitive way of working, but she finds it a challenging counterbalance to her exhibition work, and enjoys the stimulus of a focus and deadline for research. Days are spent sifting through history and art books, looking for ideas that can set off a whole chain of rough sketches, to be worked subsequently into a fully-developed design proposal.

Alice's design for the Holy Sepulchre Chapel altar frontal was intended to complement the imagery and technique of the twelfth-century wall-paintings for which the chapel is famous. The frontal's colour palette of predominantly white, silver and soft pastel shades echoes the areas of bare plaster where the paint has been lost and also the softly faded tones of much of the original painting. Occasional flashes of much brighter colour not only reflect the surprisingly strong colours which survive in the original Deposition scene above the altar but also strike a deliberately contemporary note. A lower border of gold thread lends the work a quiet radiance and, in compositional terms, forms the base of a pyramid which leads the eye through the Deposition scene to the Pantocrator, the figure of Christ in Majesty, at the apex. In this sense, the frontal becomes an integral part of the whole scheme rather than just a decorative adjunct. The main constraint for Alice lay not in acknowledging the liturgical requirements of the commission (the normal restrictions on colour dictated by the church calendar for vestments and frontals did not apply, since this frontal is expected to be in position throughout the year,) but rather in underplaying the figurative aspect which is the essence of her work. She respected the Dean and Chapter's apprehension about too literal a representation of the dead Christ by making the figure more abstract and by omitting her usual drawing lines. Interestingly, this has had an impact on her work which she is still exploring.

In the panels which Alice has been producing in 1995, such as **Basking Aphrodite VI** and **Earth Madonna**, the figures are noticeably less clearly defined than before and have a different relationship with the ground. Where they used to appear clearly delineated against the ground, they now appear to have become one with it. The faces, no longer three-dimensional, do not dominate the work and are frequently cut through. This changed relationship of figure to ground is the result of a new approach to work: Alice now starts a piece as an exercise in colour, adding the figure at a later stage. More colour can be added subsequently if needed to re-state the figure.

It is a much freer way of working and not without its anxieties:

**Altar Frontal** (1992-4)
Holy Sepulchre Chapel,
Winchester Cathedral
39" x 100" x 42", 100 x 254 x 107cm

*"It can be frightening to leave yourself with a totally jumbled-up, blank piece and wonder whether it can work, whether you can pull it all together."*

It does not mean that the figures are less important, rather the reverse. As the edges cut them through, they appear to have become larger, as if the space can no longer fully contain them. The subject now is not so much the figure as the figure and ground together, achieving greater pictorial unity.

**Glimpses of India** (1994-5)

*Detail*

With six **Glimpses of India** for the *m.v. Oriana*, Alice had imagined that it would be difficult to sustain freshness of vision when working so closely to an agreed design and over such a long period (the hangings took about twelve months to complete). In the event, however, it encouraged her to work more intuitively again as she was forced to find new ways of working in order to realise the effects in the painted designs. The project also introduced her to a different colour palette of softer tones, dictated by the fabrics chosen for the space. The dynamic of the work is not the gesture or attitude of a single figure, as in most of Alice's previous work, but the interaction between individuals in groups, and from one group to another across the large space.

The altar frontal was dedicated on Easter Saturday 1994 and the *Oriana* hangings were installed in January 1995. Since then Alice has produced a series of framed pieces in her new, more abstract style, but has yet to explore it fully in the context of a large hanging or a series of large hangings. After ten intense years of exploration, growth and consolidation, this is the challenge for the next decade which she anticipates with relish.

# WORKS AND
# ARTIST'S COMMENTARY

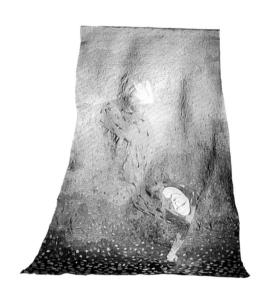

"*Eve is meant to suggest a waterfall. I tried to use the little rhythmic movements in the background to create a subtle, snakeskin pattern. Eve is seductively beautiful-serpent and jewel-like. She is beguiling as she tumbles, gently falling through space.*"

**Eve Falling from Grace** (1986)
92" x 62", 233 x 157cm
Opposite: *detail*
*Private Collection*

*"My work occupies a relaxed, middle-ground between fine and applied art. When I made the change from painting to embroidery I was aware that the two activities are closely related, but embroidery was a medium which helped me to express my individuality. We have grown up together."*

**Harlequin Madonna** (1986) *or*

**A Circle within a Square**

57" x 47", 145 x 119cm

*Collection of Bishop Otter College,*

*W. Sussex College of Education.*

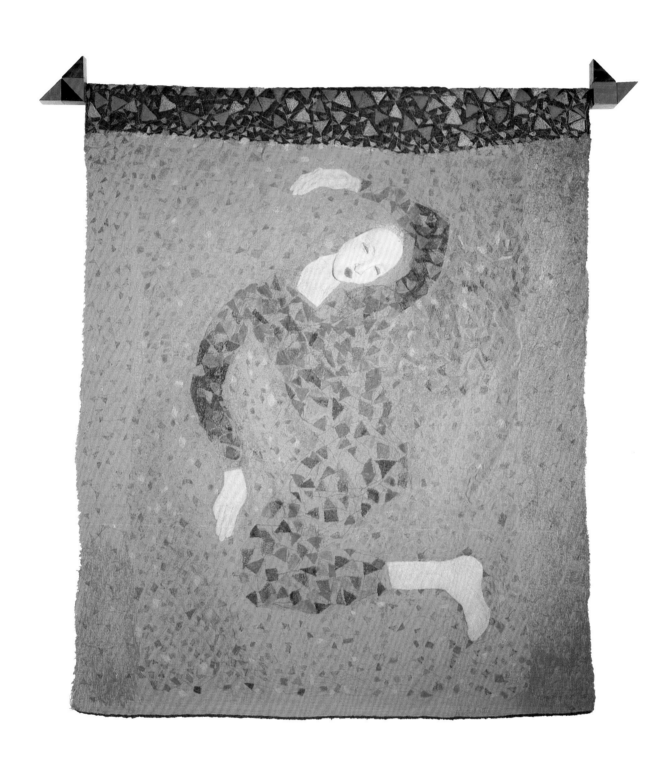

*"My interest is in the emotive power of distorted form and colour."*

**Pulchinella** (1987)
97" x 54", 247 x 136cm
Opposite: *detail*
*Private Collection*

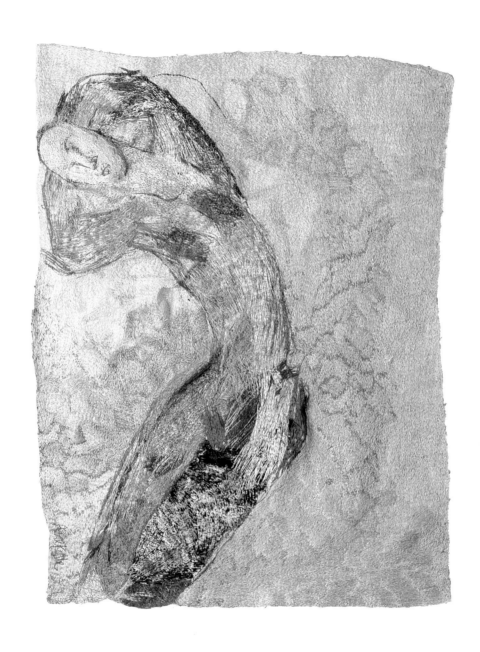

**Jumping Figure** (1987)

23" x 30", 76 x 58cm

*Private Collection*

*"I love
to watch
dancers –
they seem
to embody
so much
expression
in every
gesture."*

**Dancer II** (1988)
31" x 22", 79 x 59cm

**Arlequin sur l'Herbe** (1989)

*23" x 30", 59 x 76cm*

*"My work is a reflection of circumstance - a coming to terms with a complicated world; an illustration of my own sensibilities.*

*The pieces seek to find a harmony of mechanical process and spiritual fulfilment."*

*"Calm of the sea, imagined rest –*

*Untrue to life, yet true to love.*

*How secretly in every breast*

*The moonlit waters move."*

from *The Many-Peopled Night*
by Vernon Watkins

**Roundelay** (1989)
30" x 22", 76 x 56cm
*Private Collection*

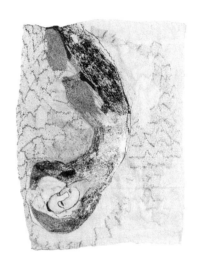

**Six Blue Nymphs** (1987-8)

each 37" x 30", 94 x 77cm

*Private Collection*

*"Black and white has so much power- it dispenses with the 'prettiness' of embroidery."*

**Anthracite II** (1989)

25" x 33", 64 x 85cm

Open University Art Collection

*"The moon has set*

*and the stars have faded,*

*midnight has gone,*

*long hours pass by, pass by;*

*I sleep alone."*

Sappho

**Red Figure** (1987)
22" x 29", 56 x 71cm
*Private Collection*

*"The theme I develop is often subconscious – it emerges in the making. I like images that are universal, that sum up some inherent quality of human existence. I like playing with contrast and paradox: these Caryatids are made of something soft, delicate and flowing, but are they stone, or even human? They are made from something intricate – but they are monumental."*

# Caryatids

Above: Pre-Classical remains at
Nemrut Dagi, central Turkey.
Opposite: **Three Caryatids,** *detail*

**Three Caryatids** (1988-9)

Three panels, each 109" x 63", 280 x 160cm

*"I relish the effect of using a precious material on such an imposing scale."*

**Indian Summer-Man** (1990)

125" x 47", 320 x 120cm

Opposite: *detail*

*"Creation is an image of man
at peace with himself and
with his surroundings.
The majestic gold columns
suggest strength, both
inner and outer strength.
The feminine is also present
in the pink and grey hues,
and in the gentle folds which
lend ambiguity to the form."*

# Creation

Above: installation of **Creation**

Southampton Central Library

Opposite: **Creation** (1991)

four panels, from left to right:

132" x 19" x 5", 335 x 50 x 14cm

117" x 38" x 2", 298 x 97 x 4cm

119" x 24" x 8", 303 x 61 x 20cm

129" x 12" x 5", 328 x 31 x 13cm

**Creation**

*Details*

*"A piece can develop from one thread."*

**Blue Basker IV** (1994)
9" x 6", 22 x 15cm

*"The brief was to create a large hanging of an angel and trumpet, which should be resonant in colour and also buoyant and floating."*

Opposite: **Angel** (1993)

86" x 63", 218 x 158cm

*Private Collection*

*"The commission brief was for six embroidered panels for the Curzon Room, a recital room named after Lord Curzon (1859-1925), a prominent Viceroy of India. The room is also used as a sitting room. I chose Indian miniatures as a starting point for my sketches.*

*Transposing a miniature onto a large format risks destroying the initial intention; so I selected certain features which I felt could translate well, such as the strong gold and the stylised layout. However I was very aware that my outlook is inevitably different from that of the Indian miniaturists. For them, their work has a specific purpose within the Hindu and Muslim faith, and an attitude to life of which I have little experience.*

# Glimpses of

**Glimpses of India** (1994-5)
Six panels, each 81" x 37", 207 x 188 cm
*believed to be the world's largest embroidery*
*designed and made by a single artist*
Opposite: panels 1, 2 and 3 in the
Curzon Room, on board *m.v. Oriana.*
Over: details of panels 6 and 2

*I had visited India a few years ago, staying with a family of painters. The visit made a deep impression on me and has fired my work for some time. But mine is a Western reaction to an exotic place: the impact of the intense and vibrant colour; the hazy shimmering light, which heightens the senses; the paradox of poverty and beauty, for me a recurrent theme - it seems to lend a poise and inner strength to the people.*

*There are paintings of the period known as Company Paintings, where Indian painters were employed by the*

# India

British "Company" to paint their chosen subjects in a style that reflects the European market. Many of them are extremely beautiful. In a sense I felt in a similar position, painting a place that has an eastern allure and exoticism to a British eye. I did not want to patronise or offend, I did want to use my own voice.

I gave the people a serene poise. They are not overtly Indian. They are mixed together in small groups, just as people sit in the room itself. They do not impose themselves on the space, they exist as a part of the whole

room. There are strong bands of gold to split up the space and to give 'glimpses' or impressions, such as one has in walking around a new place. The horizon unifies the six pieces giving a panorama of circular space. These are modern people, there is no sense of harking back.

To touch on matters of making; working to commission usually means producing designs first. This is a very different way of working from my usual approach, which is more intuitive. My work usually evolves and takes on its form in the making. I have

Above: installing **Glimpses of India**

at Meyer-Werft shipyard, Germany

Opposite: *detail of panel 2*

little idea how it will look at the end. But for commissions I have to make the most of the design stage, working with watercolour to go through this intuitive process, building up layers of colour and marks.

I paint with thread in my mind's eye, though to interpret these paintings into thread is another leap. I know how colours of thread will work together; how the colours bounce off each other. They vibrate together rather than mixing. I have to think in layers and imagine a textured, glowing surface rather than a flat surface of just colour and tone.

I suspect that I view my designs differently from those who commission them. The designs have to be a combination of my language and theirs. I was given small swatches of the fabric to be used for the interior furnishing. There was a particular shade of green that I needed to work with all the other colours and fabrics in the room – but that shade simply wasn't available in thread: so I had to use various combinations of greens, together with touches of silver, aluminium, grey, blue, copper, brown, white and black threads. I needed to achieve not only the right shade but also a wide variety of hues within the landscape represented.

To get from the designs into stitch I took slides of the painted designs and, using a slide projector, enlarged them onto the huge canvases of backing material so that I could trace the outline of the figures with a soft pencil.

This traced outline gave me an indication of the proportions, although I had to scale-up and measure very accurately, since the relative dimensions from one hanging to the next were crucial. The problem comes from stitching, which contorts and pulls the fabric, changing all those proportions. But I want the surface to be fluid so I have to accept that things will change, and be very generous with the measurements from the start.

I then start to stitch the bolder areas, working from the back with the thicker threads. All the figures and background splashes of colour are worked in this way. Then I work in the background around the figures, trying out mixtures of threads, continually reworking over places where the colours don't quite balance. And then bringing the whole together with line drawing. Finally come the heads - with them, the whole hanging is suddenly transformed, the focus changes, the lines become people.

The transition from the drawing to thread is a great leap: what was a fast brush stroke with changing colours becomes something entirely different. And yet I originally made the brushstroke with a thread in my mind's eye, so the whole thing somehow turns full circle.

Another feature of working on the pieces was that in my small studio I could not look at the pieces hanging together. A lot of the work I had to trust to my instincts."

Above: **Preliminary sketch**

Photocopy, pencil, watercolour, 5" x 7",14 x 18cm

Opposite top: **First designs**

Watercolour and pencil, 4" x 12", 10 x 30cm

Middle: **Design for panel 2**

Watercolour, 11" x 13", 28 x 33cm

Bottom: **Revised designs**

showing additional lower section

Above: **Man and Two Birds** (1992)

78" x 31", 200 x 80cm

*Detail*

Opposite: **Altar Frontal** (1992-4)

Holy Sepulchre Chapel,

Winchester Cathedral

39" x 100" x 42", 100 x 254 x 107cm

*"When I'm working I tend to think in painterly terms. But many people ask me frighteningly detailed technical questions-here is an attempt to shed some light!"*

**1** *The heads are stitched from the back, very tightly, so that the build up of thread moulds the face. There is no padding behind the faces of the framed pieces, although I sometimes use some padding for the large hangings when they are in transit for an exhibition.*

**2** *Thick, pale green rayon thread forming loose loops is caught onto the surface whilst stitching copper thread. The pale green isn't threaded through the needle and stitched, it's simply caught in place by the other stitches.*

**3** *Two fine threads, brown and copper, are stitched as one thread through the needle on the surface of the fabric. The dark green bobbin thread is very loose, pulled through to the surface of the fabric by the copper thread.*

**4** *The clothes of the figures are stitched in thick thread, wound onto the bobbin and stitched from the back. The tension of the top thread is tightened and loosened according to how much 'tufting' I want.*

**5** *The backing material used for my framed pieces is a loosely woven, neutral coloured thick fabric, one that is soft and pliable, a wool or a felt. The large unframed hangings are stitched on stiff canvas with a backing to give more body.*

**Haymakers** (1989)

11" x 20", 27 x 52cm

*Private Collection*

Opposite: *detail*

*"I know how colours of thread will work together; how the colours bounce off each other. They vibrate together rather than mixing. I have to think in layers and imagine a textured, glowing surface rather than a flat surface of just colour and tone."*

**Blue Nude V** (1993)

11" x 15", 28 x 39cm

*Private Collection*

*"I approach working on each piece in the same way as a painting, trying to make it a satisfactory piece of art, a balanced composition using line and colour."*

**Basking Aphrodite V** (1993)

13" x 17", 33 x 44cm

Private Collection

*"Working in black and white
gives me great freedom -
without decisions of colour the
line takes on paramount
importance. Black and white
brings me back to the essence
of stitch."*

**Niagra** (1995)
37" x 25", 92 x 63cm
*Private Collection*

**Magenta Basker** (1995)

7" x 9", 18 x 23cm

Opposite: **Sunbathers** (1995)

9" x 7", 23 x 18cm

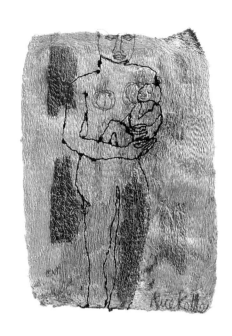

**Little Mother and Child** (1995)
7" x 5", 19 x 13cm
*Private Collection*
Opposite: **Earth Madonna** (1995)
31" x 26", 79 x 66cm
*Detail*

*"At the back of my mind were the lessons learnt from painting:-to vary the types of marks and the scale of brush strokes;-to balance bold areas with dynamic lines."*

**Basking Aphrodite VI** (1995)

13" x 17", 33 x 44cm

" ...the figure is the essence of my work, the hum

...the figure is the e...

content, the emotional link... ...

BERNINA

max. 15 W
12 V

## Training

1985-86 Goldsmiths' College,
Postgraduate Diploma, Textile Art,
with special commendation

1979-84 University of Reading,
BA (Hons) Fine Art

## Professional

1987-91 Part-time Tutor, Goldsmiths'

1987-88 Southern Arts Residency,
Cowes High School, Isle of Wight

## Visiting Lecturer

Royal College of Art, London;
Goldsmiths' College; University of Ulster;
Embroiderers' Guild, London;
Chelsea School of Art; W. Sussex College
of Further Education; Knuston Hall; Stitch
Design, London; Quarry Bank Mill, Styal;
Aspex Gallery, Portsmouth.

## Grants and Awards

1993 Cosmopolitan Achievement Awards,
(special commendation in
Creative Arts Category)

1992 Marketing Grant, Southern Arts

1991 British Council Grant

1991 Southern Arts Grant

1988 Training Scheme, Crafts Council

1988 Southern Arts Grant

1988 Taittinger Prize

1987 Setting Up Grant, Crafts Council

1987 Southern Arts Grant

1985 Clothworkers' Foundation Grant

## Membership

Fellow of Society of Designer-Craftsmen
Friend of '62 Group of Textile Artists

..the figure is the essence of my work, the human

## Public and Corporate Commissions

1994-5 **Glimpses of India**, *mv Oriana*, commissioned by P&O Cruises, (UK) Ltd.

1994 **Altar Frontal**, Holy Sepulchre Chapel, Winchester Cathedral, commissioned by the Dean and
Chapter, part-funded by Southern Arts with supplementary donations
from Shoei College and private benefactors. Madeira Threads supplied materials at reduced price.

1992 **Overtures of Gold**, commissioned by Open University Faculty of Arts.

1991 **The Saga of McGuinness's Dog**, commissioned by Southern Arts for Bernard O'Donoghue,
winner of 1991 Southern Arts Poetry Prize.

1989 **Banner** for Aspex Gallery, Portsmouth.

**Public & Corporate Collections** with date of installation

1995 **Creation**, Southampton Central Library, NorthGuild, Civic Centre

1993 **Two Harlequins**, The Prudential, Reading

1992 **Three Caryatids**, The Whitworth Art Gallery, Manchester. Acquired jointly by Victoria & Albert
    Museums and Galleries Commission Purchase Grant Fund, and by the Friends of the Whitworth

1992 **Anthracites I & II**, on loan to Open University Art Collection, Milton Keynes,
    from the collection of the late Mrs Angela Trew

1990 **Melisande**, Portsmouth City Museum & Art Gallery

1990 **Stretching Figure**, Crafts Council Collection, London

1988 **Arethusa**, The Broadgate Club, London EC1

1987 **Tranquil Figure**, Embroiderers' Guild Textile Collection, Hampton Court Palace

1987 **Harlequin Madonna**, W. Sussex College Collection, Chichester

*...ontent, the emotional link... ...the figure is the ess*

**Selected Illustrated Press Articles**

Anne Morrell, Machine Embroidery, **Textiles** Volume 24,1995 • Ruth Pavey, Oriana, **Crafts**, July 1995
Cruise Lines Leave the Doldrums, **Independent on Sunday** 19.3.95 • Alice Makes Mark on 21st Century
Art with World's Biggest Embroidery, **Hampshire Chronicle** 20.1.95 • Embroidery Drawing,
**Country Living**, April 1994 • Margot Coatts, Alice in Winchester, **Crafts** November 1994 • Alison Roberts,
P&O Push The Boat Out For Artists, **The Times**, 10.5.94 • Artist Echoes a Medieval Tradition, **Hampshire
Chronicle**, April 94 • Tom Lundberg, Swatches, **Fibre Arts**, USA, Summer 1993 • **Textilforum**, Holland,
Summer 1993 • International Showcase, **Beautiful Home**, Hong Kong, September 1992 • Margot Coatts,
Material Advances, **Crafts**, September 1992 • Audrey Walker, In Context, **Embroidery**, Spring 1992 •
Elizabeth Benn, Spotlight on Alice Kettle, **Embroidery**, Summer 1992 • Chelsea's Choice, **Crafts**,
September 1991 • Dominique Vollichard, Alice Kettle a Filambule, **24 Heures**, Lausanne, Switzerland,
30.4.91 • Alice Kettle, **NeedleArts** USA, December 1990 • Shining Kettle, **Interior (International
Textiles)**,1988 no. 3 • Emma Bernhardt, Pure Fabrications, **Elle Magazine**, February 1988 • Alice Kettle,
A Formal Image, **Embroidery**, Autumn 1987 • Anthea Godfrey, Embroidery at the RIBA,
**Embroidery**, Winter 1986

## Exhibition List (selected)

1996    William Morris Revisited, Whitworth Art Gallery,
Manchester; Crafts Council, London;
Birmingham Museum and Art Gallery (tour)
Hipotesi Gallery, Barcelona
Scottish Gallery, Edinburgh

1995    CCA Galleries, Cambridge with
Jeanette Appleton and Alison King
Art-in-Action, Waterperry House, Oxford
Smith's Gallery, Covent Garden, London
Decorative Arts Today, Bonhams, London
Embroiderers' Guild Open Exhibition, Commonwealth
Institute, London, and Whitworth Art Gallery
AIM Summer Show, Milton Keynes
Quarry Bank Mill, Styal
Studio sale, Winchester,
with Sarah Brooker and Augusta Wolff
Idea and Image, Newbury Spring Festival

1994    Decorative Arts Today, Bonhams, London
Winchester Contemporary Art
NorthGuild Gallery Shop, Southampton Civic Centre
Oxford Gallery, with Louise Baldwin
Summer Show, Contemporary Applied Arts
AIM Summer Show, Milton Keynes

Visions of Crafts, Highlights from the
Crafts Council Collection

1993    Decorative Arts Today, Bonhams, London
Figurative Embroidered Textiles, City Gallery, Leicester
Chelsea Crafts Fair, London
Summer Show, Contemporary Applied Arts
Christmas Exhibition, Reeves Yard, Norwich
Herbert Art Gallery & Museum, Coventry
Money and Art, The Whitworth Art Gallery, Manchester

1992    Out of the Frame, Crafts Council, London; Aberystwyth
Arts Centre; Plymouth City Museum; Wakefield
Art Gallery: Peter Scott Gallery, Lancaster (tour)
Salisbury Playhouse (solo)
Contemporary Textile Gallery
Decorative Arts Today, Bonhams, London
Studio sale, Winchester,
with Csilla Kelecsényi and Augusta Wolff
'62 Group 30th Anniversary Exhibition,
Commonwealth Institute, London
'62 Group Exhibition, Hankyu Dpt Stores, Osaka, Japan

1991    Galerie Filambule, Lausanne, Switzerland (solo)
Can't Stop Me Now!, Crafts Council, London (tour)
'62 Group Exhibition, Bluecoat Display Centre, Liverpool
Chelsea Crafts Fair, London
Hitchcock's, Alresford, Hampshire
Favourite Things, Crafts Council Gallery, London

1990    Stitched Textiles - a Celebration, Embroiderers' Guild
Exhibition, Commonwealth Institute, London
Cross Threads, Bradford Textiles Festival (tour)
My Eyes, Your Hands, Brewery Arts Centre, Kendal (solo)
Scottish Gallery, Edinburgh (solo)

1989    Machinations, Howard Gardens Gallery, Cardiff
(2 person tour with Sarah Brooker)
11 from '62 in '89 - Textiles, Turnpike Gallery, Leigh
Cirencester Workshops
Dundee College of Art
Portsmouth City Art Gallery
New Faces, Crafts Council Shop at the V&A, London
Parnham House, Somerset
Black Swan Guild, Frome, Somerset
Chelsea Crafts Fair, London

1988    Alice Kettle - Showcase, ICA, London (solo)
Figure Happy, Midlands Arts Centre, Birmingham (tour)
The Gantry, Southampton (solo)
Tex-styles, Smith's Gallery, Covent Garden, London

Oxford Gallery (solo)
Quay Arts Centre, Newport, Isle of Wight (solo)
Winchester People's Pageant

1987    Material Images, Howard Gardens Gallery, Cardiff
Paintings & Textiles, Oxford Gallery (solo)
British Design Centre
'62 Group, Contemporary Textile Gallery, London
Thamesday Exhibition, Southbank Centre, London
Young Designers, Contemporary Textile Gallery, London
W. Sussex College of Higher Education, Chichester (solo)
Stitchery International, Pittsburgh, USA
Chelsea Crafts Fair, London
'62 Group, City Gallery, Leicester
Winchester Design Workshops, Hitchcocks', Bath

1986    Stitched Textiles for Interiors, RIBA Gallery, London
Contemporary Textile Gallery, London
Oxford Gallery (solo)

*...the figure is the essence of my work, the human*

# Bibliography

*The Oriana Collection*
P&O Cruises (UK), Ltd, 1995

*5000 Years of Embroidery*
Ed. Jennifer Harris
British Museum Publications 1993

*Contemporary Embroidery*
Anne Morrell
Cassell 1993

*Drawing, Seeing and Observation*
Ian Simpson
A&C Black, 1992

*The New Textiles*
Chloe Colchester
Thames & Hudson 1992

*Stitch Images 2 (Video)*
Southern Arts, 1990

*Designer Textiles*
The Embroiderers' Guild
David & Charles 1987

*...ntent, the emotional link... ..the figure is the esse*

ce of my work, the human content, the emotional

...the figure is 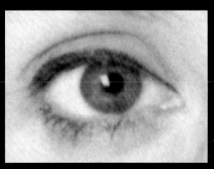 the essence of my

# Index of Works

# Acknowledgments

*"This book is dedicated in love to the memory of my Mother and Father."*

The artist wishes to thank all the many people who have generously given their support and encouragement over the years, and in particular Audrey Walker, Professor Anne Morrell, Linda Theophilus, David Kay and Gay Daniels. With thanks to Elizabeth Jennings and Penguin Books for kind permission to reproduce an extract from *The Counterpart*; to Gwen Watkins and Golgonooza Press for permission to reproduce extracts from *The Collected Poems* of Vernon Watkins; and to translator Josephine Balmer and Brilliance Books for permission to reproduce an extract from Sappho *'Poems and Fragments'*. Permission to reproduce photography is acknowledged with thanks to Theo Hodges & P&O page 3; P&O page 58; The Crafts Council pages 34, 35; The Whitworth Art Gallery page 14; Crafts Magazine page 45. With thanks to the following for making work available to be photographed: Robert Bottone, Gay Daniels, Jean Draper, Dr Lesley Forrest, Meg and John Gammell, Peta Levi MBE, Sarah and Glen Miller, Carol Naylor, Lindsay Nevin, P&O Cruises (UK) Ltd, Rosemary Smith, Diana Springall, Canon Walker. Additional photography by: Mike O'Dwyer pages 3, 7, 25, 26, 27, 64; Michael Harvey page 19, 65; Hugh Kelley pages 47, 53, 81; Dudley Moss page 13; James Newell pages 18, 48; the artist pages 10, 40, 46. All other photographs by James Johnson. The editor wishes to thank in particular Keiren Phelan, Tim Earnshaw, Samantha Taylor, Janet Summerton, Carol Pusey and Miranda McKearney for their help.